# 108 QUOTES

## on

## LOVE

*Amma*

Aunt Lisa,
Thank you so much for
sharing your home with us. It made for
a beautiful adventure! May you be well
and feel Amma's love!
♡ Thank you ♡
Thomas and Hannah

# 108 QUOTES ON LOVE

Published by:
Mata Amritanandamayi Mission Trust
Amritapuri P.O., Kollam Dt., Kerala
INDIA 690525
Email: inform@amritapuri.org
Website: www.amritapuri.org

Typesetting and layout by Amrita DTP, Amritapuri

First edition: April 2014

1

Love is our true essence. Love has no limitations of caste, religion, race, or nationality. We are all beads strung together on the same thread of love. To awaken this unity and spread the love that is our inherent nature, is the true goal of human life.

## 2

'Am I really in love, or am I too attached?' Contemplate on this question as deeply as you can. Most people are craving for attachment, not real love. In a way, we are betraying ourselves. We mistake attachment for love. Love is the centre and attachment is the periphery. Aim for the centre.

## 3

Beauty lies in the heart. Love towards everyone gives real beauty, enhancing both the giver as well as the receiver. The loveliness of our eyes is not in the eye-liner, but in a compassion filled glance. The smile that lights up a face brimming with love is the most beautiful in the whole world.

4

$M$ost of us are always thinking about the losses in life. We forget about the greatest gain that we can have – that is love. Let your mind open up fully, and you will experience love with all its fragrance and beauty.

5

Love is the foundation of a happy life, but consciously or unconsciously we forget this truth. When we do not express love in our words and actions, it is like honey trapped in a rock — it is of no use to anyone. When families are able to express love with each other, peace and harmony will prevail in the home and in society.

# 6

When you see others as you see yourself, there is no individuality. Compassion is the language the blind can see and the deaf can hear. Lending a helping hand to a neglected soul, feeding the hungry, giving the sad and dejected a compassionate glance – this is the language of love.

7

If we pour our heart and soul into an activity, it will be transformed into a tremendous source of inspiration. The product of an action performed with love will have a discernable presence of light and life in it. That reality of love will fill people's minds with immense attraction.

# 8

Behind all great and unforgettable events is the heart. Love and a selfless attitude underlie all truly great deeds. Behind any good cause, you will find somebody who has renounced everything and dedicated his or her life to it.

# 9

When we realise that all love – whether from a husband, wife, child, animal rearing its young, or a plant – is from the one and only Divine source, then our love will begin to radiate light and coolness just like moonlight. Cultivating this understanding will bring harmony to our lives.

Find your inner harmony, that beautiful song of life and love. Reach out and serve the suffering. Learn to place others before yourself. But in the name of serving others, do not fall in love with your own ego. Be a master of your mind and ego. Consider everyone, because they are each a doorway to your own Self.

Work can be exhausting and dissipate our energy, whereas love is never tiring or boring. Love fills our hearts with more and more energy. It makes everything eternally new and fresh. When our existence is rooted in pure love, how can we ever be bored? Boredom only comes in the absence of love. Love fills life constantly with newness.

## 12

If there is true love, nothing else is needed. That itself leads to complete absorption. As we develop love and intent towards the goal, we will automatically forgive and forget; we will be able to imbibe the attitude of sacrifice.

13

The more dedicated you are, the more open you become. The more open you remain, the more love you experience. The more love you give, the more grace you receive. It is this grace that will bring you to the goal.

## 14

Pure love is a constant giving up — giving up everything that belongs to you. Yet, what really belongs to you? — Only the ego. Love consumes in its flames all preconceived ideas, prejudices and judgments — all those things that stem from the ego.

## 15

Realise that infinite bliss is within your Self.
When the love that is within you expresses itself
in external activities, you will experience true
happiness.

When you are happy, your heart is open, and Divine love can flow into you. When love is enshrined within, you will only be happy. It is a cycle; happiness draws love inside, and love allows you to be happy.

17

If we dive deep enough inside ourselves, we will find that the same thread of universal love ties all beings together. It is love that unites everything.

## 18

One drop of water cannot be called a river; a river is formed by many drops running together. It is the joining of these countless drops that creates the flow. Together we are a power, an undefeatable power. When we work together, hand in hand, with love, it is not just one life force but the life energy of the collective that flows in harmony, unimpeded. From that constant stream of unity, we will see the birth of peace.

## 19

Whenever you go through a difficult time in life, it is good to remind yourself, 'I don't expect any love from others because I am not someone who needs to be loved by others. I am love itself. I am an inexhaustible source of love, who will always give love, and nothing but love, to everyone who comes to me.'

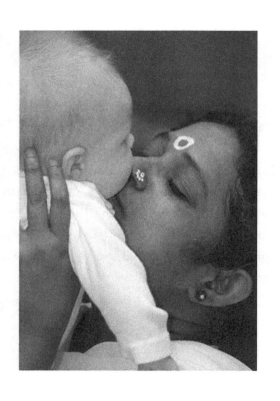

True love cannot be rejected. You can only receive it with an open heart. When a child smiles, whether it is the child of your friend or of a foe, you cannot help but smile back because the child's love is so pure and innocent. Pure love is like a beautiful flower with an irresistible fragrance.

The power of pure love is infinite. In true love, one goes beyond the body, mind and all fears. Love is the breath of the soul. It is our life force. Pure, innocent love makes everything possible. When your heart is filled with the pure energy of love, even the most impossible task is as easy as picking up a flower.

The more love you give, the more divinity is expressed within you. Just as water from a perennial spring never dries up no matter how much we draw from it, the more kindness we give, the more it increases.

Life and love are not two; they are inseparable like a word and its meaning. We take birth in love, lead this life in love and at last get merged in love. The truth is: there is no end for love. Only through love can life spring forth and flower. As love is our innate nature, there cannot be a manifestation of any kind without this power behind it.

## 24

Love can accomplish anything. There is no problem that love cannot solve. It can cure diseases, heal wounded hearts and transform minds. Through love one can overcome all obstacles. Love can help us renounce all physical, mental and intellectual tensions, thereby bringing peace and happiness. Love is the ambrosia that adds beauty and charm to life.

Love is a universal religion. It is what society really needs. It should be expressed in all of our words and deeds. Love and spiritual values received from parents are the strongest assets that a child needs in order to face the various trials of adulthood.

## 26

In a perfect relationship between humanity and nature, a circular energy field is created in which both start flowing into each other. When we human beings fall in love with nature, she will fall in love with. She will stop hiding things from us. Opening her infinite treasure trove, she will allow us to enjoy her wealth. Like a mother, she will protect, nurture and nourish us.

## 27

When we love one another without any expectation, there is no need to go anywhere else in search of heaven. Love is the foundation of a happy life. Just like our bodies need proper food to live and grow, our souls are nourished by love.

## 28

We cannot change the nature of others through anger. Only love can change them. Understand this and try to have sympathy and love for everyone. Be compassionate even towards those who irritate you. Try to pray for them. Such an attitude will help your mind remain peaceful and calm. As one changes for the better, the action–reaction patterns loosen, and the heart opens more to positive qualities such as forgiveness, tolerance and harmony.

## 29

It is through selfless sharing that the flower of life becomes beautiful and fragrant. When a flower blossoms, its sweet fragrance spreads all around. Likewise, when selfless love awakens within us, it flows to the world like a river.

## 30

Within you, there is a wellspring of love. Tap that source in the right way, and the Divine energy of love will fill your heart, expanding endlessly. You cannot make it happen; you can only create the right attitude within yourself and it will happen naturally.

Real love exists in the heart. This love cannot be spoken or even put into words. Words belong to the intellect. Go beyond the words and language into the heart. When one really loves, one's intellect becomes empty; one stops thinking — no thoughts, no mind, nothing. Only love remains.

32

Love and beauty are within you. Try to express them through your actions, and you will definitely touch the very source of bliss.

## 33

Do your work and perform your duties with all your heart. Try to work selflessly with love. When you pour yourself into everything that you do, you will feel and experience beauty and love in all your actions.

## 34

The goal of spirituality is to change our limited love into Divine love. Therefore, let us focus on what we can give to others and not what we can take for ourselves. This will bring about great transformation in our lives.

## 35

Whether it is spiritual love or worldly love, love remains love. The difference is only in depth and degree. Spiritual love is without limits or boundaries, while worldly love is superficial and limited. Awaken to the knowledge, 'I am the Supreme Self; I am unlimited, and I have infinite potential inside me.'

# 36

If the sun shines down into a thousand different pots filled with water, the reflections are many, but they are each reflecting the same sun. Similarly, if we come to know who we truly are, we will see ourselves in all people. When this understanding arises, we learn to consider others, overlooking their weaknesses. From that, pure love will dawn from within.

## 37

The love of awakened motherhood is a love and compassion felt not only towards one's own children, but towards all people, animals, plants, rocks and rivers – a love extended to all of nature, all beings. Anyone – woman or man – who has the courage to overcome the limitations of the mind can attain this state of universal motherhood.

## 38

Love cannot contain two. It only contains one. In love's constant and devoted remembrance, 'you' and 'I' disappear and dissolve. Love alone remains. The entire universe is contained in that pure, undivided love. Love is endless; nothing can be excluded from it.

# 39

The difficulty is not in expressing love, but in letting go of the ego. Love is our true nature. It is already present within us, but we are held back by our individual boundaries. We have to outgrow our individuality in order to merge into universal love. The ego stands in the way of love. Once it is removed, we will flow like a river.

Your heart is the real temple. You must install God there. Good thoughts are the flowers to be offered; good actions are worship; good words are hymns. Love is the divine offering.

# 41

There is an insatiable hunger in pure love. One can see and experience this intense hunger even in worldly love, but in spiritual love the intensity reaches its peak. In a true seeker, love becomes like a forest fire, but even more consuming. Our whole being burns with the intensity of the fire of love. In that blazing fire, we ourselves get consumed and then completely merge in the Divine.

# 42

Love is not something that can be taught by someone or learned from somewhere, but in the presence of a perfect Master we can feel it and, in due course, develop it. This is because a Satguru (true Guru) creates the necessary circumstances for love to grow within us. The situations created by the Guru will be so beautiful and unforgettable that we will truly cherish these precious and invaluable moments. They will remain as sweet memories forever.

# 43

Incidents created by the Guru will make a chain of exhilarating memories that will produce waves and waves of love within us, until at last there will be only love. Through these circumstances the Guru will steal our heart and soul, filling us with pure and innocent love.

# 44

There is 'love' and Love. You love your family: your father, mother, sister, brother, husband, wife, etc; but you do not love your neighbour. You love your son or daughter, but you do not love all children. You love your religion, but you do not love all religions. Likewise, you have love for your country, but you do not love all countries. Hence, this is not Love; it is only 'love.' Transformation of this 'love' to Love is the goal of spirituality.

# 45

Love just happens as a sudden rising in the heart; as an unavoidable, unobstructed longing for oneness. Nobody thinks about how to love, or when and where to love. Rational thought hinders love. Love is beyond logic, so do not try to be rational about love. That is like trying to give reasons for the river to flow, for the breeze to be cool and gentle, for the moon to glow, for the sky to be expansive, for the ocean to be vast and deep, or for the flower to be fragrant and beautiful. Rationalisation kills the beauty and charm of these things. They are to be enjoyed, experienced, loved and felt. If you rationalise about them, you will miss the beauty and charm of the feelings that love evokes.

# 46

The responsibility of a mother cannot be underestimated. A mother has immense influence over her children. When we see happy, peaceful individuals; children endowed with noble qualities and good disposition; men who have immense strength when faced with failure and adverse situations; people who possess great measures of understanding, sympathy, love and compassion towards the suffering; and those who give of themselves to others, we will usually find a great mother who has inspired them to become what they are.

# 47

Mothers are most able to sow the seeds of love, universal kinship and patience in our minds. There is a special bond between a mother and a child. The mother's inner qualities are transmitted to the child even through her breast milk. The mother understands the heart of the child; she pours her love into the child, teaches the positive lessons of life and corrects the child's mistakes.

## 48

May the tree of our life be firmly rooted in the soil of love. May good deeds be the leaves on that tree. May words of kindness form its flowers, and may peace be its fruit. Let us grow and unfold as one family united in love.

# 49

Finding one's true Self and loving everyone equally are the same thing. Only when you learn to love everyone equally will true freedom emerge. Until then you are bound; you are the slave to the ego and the mind.

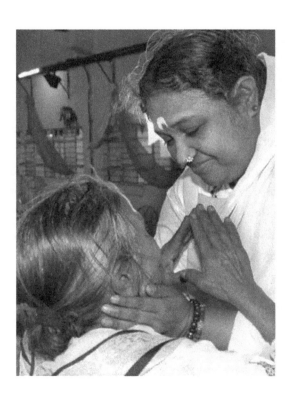

# 50

Just as the body needs food to survive and grow, the soul needs love. Love instills a strength and vitality that even mother's milk cannot provide. We all live for and long for real love. We are born and die searching for such love. Children, love each other and unite in this pure love.

No one loves anyone more than they love themselves. Behind everyone's love is a selfish search for their own happiness. When we do not get the happiness that we expect from a friend, our friend becomes our enemy. This is what can be seen in the world. Only God loves us selflessly. It is only through loving the Divine that we can learn to love and serve others selflessly.

# 52

Pure love is the best medicine for the modern world. This is what is lacking in all societies. The root cause of all problems, from personal to global, is the absence of love. Love is the binding factor, the unifying force in everything. Love creates feelings of oneness and unity among people, while hatred and egotism cause division and cut people's minds into pieces. Love should rule. There is no problem that love cannot solve.

# 53

In order to develop love, one should be in a suitable place for love to grow. To live in the presence of a perfect Master is the best way to develop love. The Guru helps you by creating the circumstances necessary to fill your heart with love. These circumstances are not only external, but internal as well. The Guru works directly with the disciple's vasanas (latent tendencies), which stand as the main obstacles on the path of love.

# 54

Real growth takes place in the unity that is born out of love. The milk that flows out of the mother's breast nourishes the baby and provides its body with strength and vitality, allowing all of the organs to grow healthily and in proportion. But, it is not just milk that flows out of the mother's breast; it is the warmth, the love and the affection of the mother in the form of milk. In a similar way, love is the 'breast milk' that helps society to grow as a whole. Love provides the necessary strength and vitality that enables society to grow without division.

# 55

Mahatmas are the bridge joining us to God. They do not reject anything. They are like a river; embracing and accepting everything as it flows. Pleasure and pain are like the two shores of life. Mahatmas accept both these banks with equanimity and move forward. At the same time, they are beyond thoughts and emotions. They are attached to everyone, yet bound by nothing. A heart that is full of love and faith will easily establish a bond with them.

56

The powers of unshakable faith and innocent love can penetrate into realms where intellect and logic cannot enter.

# 57

You can only feel love by expressing it. The reason why we practice spirituality is to learn how to forgive others for their mistakes and to love them instead of rejecting them. Anyone can reject people, but to accept everyone is difficult. Through love we can lead others from wrong to right, whereas if we disown someone for their mistakes, they may continue to commit them.

# 58

We love others because they give us happiness or fulfil our desires; obeying, respecting or having a high opinion about us. Otherwise, we do not love them. If somebody hates us, revenge often takes the place of love. This is the case even with those closest to you. If they disobey or disrespect you, you may not love them. Where there is real love, there is no selfishness. We must be able to love without expecting anything from anyone.

# 59

When there is no more aversion or hostility — that is love. When every aversion disappears from the mind, the mind transforms into love. It becomes like sugar: anyone can come and take from it, enjoying its sweetness without having to give anything in return. When you can love and serve humanity, you become food for the world.

# 60

Children, Divine love is our true nature. It is shining in each and every one of us. When your heart is full of innocent love, you are absent; the ego is absent. In that state, only love is present; individuality disappears, and you become one with the Divine.

When a child offers something, it cannot be rejected because a child's love is untainted and pure. When you dwell in authentic, innocent love, there are no dual feelings like purity or impurity, good or bad, and so forth. There is only love. Pure love cannot be rejected.

# 62

Love just flows. Whoever is willing to take the plunge and dive in, will be accepted as they are. There are no terms or conditions. If you are not willing to jump in, what can love do? The stream remains where it is. It never says, 'No.' It is constantly saying, 'Yes, yes, yes.'

# 63

When you open up, you will find that the sun was always shining and the wind always blowing, carrying the sweet fragrance of Divine love. There are no conditions; no force being used. Just allow the door of your heart to open and you will find that it was never locked. This door has always been open, but in your ignorance you thought it was locked.

# 64

Real love arises only when all attachments to individuals, objects and interests drop away. Then the battle becomes a beautiful play of selfless service, extended towards the entire human race out of love and compassion. In that fighting, your ego will not fight, but love will fight to consume the ego and transform it into love. The shadow of fear disappears only in the light of love.

# 65

In this age of intellect and reason, the age of science, we have forgotten the feelings of the heart. A common expression all over the world is, 'I have fallen in love.' Yes, we have fallen down into a love rooted in selfishness and materialism. We are unable to arise and awaken in love. If we must fall, let it be from the head to the heart. Rising up in Love – that is spirituality.

# 66

When we have love for something, an incessant and unbroken stream of thought flows towards that object. Our thoughts are only about that. Therefore, to really love we need concentration, and to really concentrate, we need to love the object, whatever it may be. One cannot exist without the other. A scientist who does experiments in the laboratory needs a lot of concentration. Where does this concentration come from? From his deep and intense interest in that subject. From where does this deep interest come? It is the result of intense love that he has towards his particular subject or field of study. Conversely, if one concentrates on a subject intensely, love for it will also develop.

# 67

We should try to see the nature of things as they are. The nature of anything, whether an object or a person, cannot be other than the way it is. If this is understood, we can truly respond rather than react. Through our anger, we cannot change the nature of others. Only love can change them. Understand this and pray for their good with sympathy and love. Try to be compassionate, even towards those who upset you. Such an attitude will help your mind to be calm and peaceful. This is genuine response.

# 68

What is impure should become pure. All impurity should melt and disappear in the heat brought on by the pain of separation and longing for Divine love. This suffering is known as tapas. The gopis became totally identified with Krishna through this pain. Their anguish was so excruciating and intense that their individuality disappeared completely, and they merged with their beloved Krishna. Impurity is caused by the feelings of 'I' and 'mine,' which are the ego. The ego cannot be eradicated unless one burns it in the furnace of love.

# 69

Real love is experienced when there are no conditions. Where love is present, nothing can be forced; force is only used when we perceive others to be different from ourselves. Conditional love cannot exist when there is only oneness. The very idea of force disappears in that state. Then you simply are. The universal life energy flows through you when you become an open passage. Let the Supreme Consciousness take charge, removing obstructions to its flow, allowing the river of all-embracing love to run its course.

# 70

In authentic love, there is no attachment. One has to transcend all petty human feelings in order to attain Supreme love. In other words, love dawns only when detachment arises. Love involves a tremendous amount of self-sacrifice. At certain points it may cause great pain, but authentic love always culminates in everlasting bliss.

In pure love, there is no burden. Nothing can be a burden when there is love without desire. Real love can carry the entire universe without feeling any weight. Compassion can shoulder the suffering of the entire world without feeling the slightest bit of pain.

God is the only one who truly loves us without expecting anything in return. Children, even if all the creatures in the whole world love us, it cannot equal even a fraction of the love that we experience from God in every second. There is no other love that can compare to God's love.

# 73

In the final stage of love, the lover and the beloved become one. Even beyond this, there comes a state where there is no love, lover or beloved. That ultimate state of Love is beyond expression. This is where the Master finally takes you.

# 74

A beautiful melody emerging from a flute is neither to be found in the flute nor in the player's fingertips. You could say it comes from the composer's heart, yet if you were to open up his heart and take a look, you would not find it there either. What then is the original source of the music? The source is beyond; it emerges out of the Paramatman (Supreme Self), but the ego cannot recognise this power. Only if you learn to function from the heart can you really see and feel the power of the Divine in your life.

## 75

A flower does not need instructions on how to bloom. No music teacher taught the nightingale to sing. It is spontaneous. There is no force involved; it happens naturally. Similarly, in the presence of a great Master, the closed bud of your heart opens up. You become as receptive and innocent as a child. The Master does not teach you anything; you learn everything without being taught. His presence, his very life, is the greatest teaching of all. There is no control or force involved; everything happens naturally and effortlessly. Only love can create this miracle.

# 76

A rishi (saint) never creates division in life. This makes him truly able to love because he has delved into the mysteries of his own Self, the very core of life and love. He experiences life and love everywhere. For him there is nothing but life and love shining forth with splendour and glory. Therefore, he is the 'real scientist.' He experiments in the inner laboratory of his own being and always dwells in an undivided state of love.

When there are no desires, there is no sorrow. We must be able to love everyone without expecting anything in return. It is not easy to love everybody, but at least we can try not to be angry at people or hurt them. We can start from that level. Imagine that each person is sent by God, and you will be able to be kind and loving to everyone.

# 78

A spiritual person should become like the wind. Feeling life's oneness broadens our minds, expands our hearts and spreads love to all of creation. The first requirement, along with remembrance of God, is to love everyone and everything, both sentient and insentient. If we have that greatness of heart, liberation will not be far behind.

Pure love transcends the body. It is between hearts; it has nothing to do with bodies. When there is true love, there are no barriers and no limitations. Even though the sun is far away, the lotus flowers still bloom in its effulgence. In true love, there is no distance.

Love is the only language that every living being can understand. It is universal. Peace and love are the same for everyone. Like honey, love is always sweet. Be like the honeybee that gathers the nectar of love wherever it goes. Seek the goodness in everyone and everything.

There are three expressions of love that awaken us from within: love for oneself, love for God, and love for the entire creation. Love for oneself does not mean the self-centred love of the ego. It means to love life, to see both the successes and failures in our human birth as God's blessing, while loving the Divine power inherent within us. This grows to become love for God. If these two components are present, then the third component, love for the entire creation, will manifest naturally.

The heart alone can guide a person, but the heart has been forgotten. In reality, love has no form. Only when love constantly flows through a person does it assume a form that we will be able to experience; otherwise we cannot. When someone's heart is filled with love and compassion, your own heart will spontaneously open up like a blossoming flower. The closed bud of your heart unfolds in the presence of love.

# 83

Love cannot force. Love is the presence of pure consciousness; that presence cannot force. It simply is. The energy of pure love is within you; it only needs to awaken.

# 84

The spirit of worldly love is not constant. Its rhythm fluctuates; it comes and goes. The beginning is always beautiful and enthusiastic, but slowly it gets less beautiful and less exciting until it ends up becoming shallow. In most cases, worldly love ends in upset, hatred and deep sorrow. On the contrary, spiritual love is as deep as a bottomless pit; its depth and expansiveness cannot be measured.

# 85

Spiritual love is different than worldly love. The beginning is beautiful and peaceful. Shortly after this peaceful beginning comes the agony of longing. Through the middle period, the agony will continue to grow stronger and stronger, more and more unbearable. Excruciating pain will ensue, and this pain of longing will remain until just before achieving unity with the beloved. This unity is even more inexpressibly beautiful than the beginning of love. Love of this kind never dries up or diminishes. Spiritual love is always alive, both within and without; it is constant, and each moment you live in love.

# 86

Love will swallow you. It will eat you up completely until there is no 'you,' and there is only love. Your whole being will be transformed into love. Spiritual love culminates in unity, in oneness.

God dwells deep within our hearts as innocence and pure love. We should learn to love everyone equally and express this love, because in essence we are all one, one Atman, one soul. Love is the face of God.

## 88

The essence of motherhood is not restricted to women who have given birth; it is a principle inherent in both women and men. It is an attitude of the mind. It is love — and that love is the very breath of life. When our sense of universal motherhood has awakened, love and compassion for everyone are as much a part of our being as breathing.

# 89

Love sustains everything. If we penetrate deeply into all aspects and areas of life, we will find that hidden beneath everything is love. We will discover that love is the power, the energy and the inspiration behind every word and action.

## 90

When you learn to love everyone equally, genuine freedom will emerge. Without love there can be no freedom, and without freedom, there can be no love. Eternal freedom can happen only when all our negativity has been uprooted. In that state of all-encompassing love the beautiful, fragrant flower of freedom and Supreme bliss can unfold its petals and blossom.

# 91

As love becomes more subtle, it gains power. As it goes deeper into the depths of the heart, you will find that you are rising in love. Finally you will reach the state of total identification with the Beloved where you realise that you are not separate. This is when you become one. It is the ultimate step, and the height of real love. It is where love should be taking us.

# 92

We are all embodiments of Supreme Love. Love can be compared to a ladder. Most people stay on the bottom rung. Do not remain there. Keep climbing, one step at a time. Ascend from the lowest rung to the highest, from the level of emotion to the highest state of being, the purest form of love.

# 93

True love is the purest form of energy. In that state, love is not an emotion; it is a constant flow of genuine awareness and unlimited power. Such love can be compared to our breath. You never say, 'I will breathe only in front of my family and relatives, never in front of my enemies or those I hate.' — No. Wherever you are, whatever you are doing, breathing just happens. In a similar manner, true love gives to everyone without any difference, expecting nothing in return. Become a giver, not a taker.

# 94

It is the care and patience we show in small things that lead us to great achievements. If you have patience, then you will also have love. Patience leads to love. If you forcefully open the petals of a budding flower, you will not be able to enjoy its splendour and perfume. Only when it blossoms naturally will its loveliness and fragrance unfold. Likewise, you need to have patience to enjoy the beauty in life.

# 95

The earring, the bangle, the nose-ring and the necklace – in essence, all are gold alone; only their appearance is different. Similarly, it is one all-pervasive Divinity appearing as this diverse world of names and forms. When we truly understand this truth, it is reflected in all our thoughts, words and actions as love, compassion and selflessness.

# 96

Extending help without expecting anything in return is real service. It is the power that sustains the world. To love and serve with dedication can be compared to a circle, for a circle has no beginning or end. Love does not have a beginning or end either. Through selfless service, we can construct a bridge of love to bring us all together.

No work is insignificant or meaningless. The amount of love and awareness that you pour into your work makes it significant and beautiful. Grace flows into work done with humility. Humility infuses it with sweetness.

## 98

Like love, surrender cannot be studied or learned from books, from a particular person or from a university. Surrender comes as love grows. In fact, the two grow simultaneously. Ultimately, we must surrender to our own true Self, but surrender requires a lot of courage. We need a daring attitude to sacrifice our ego. This requires us to welcome and accept everything without any feelings of sorrow or disappointment.

The intellect and the heart should come together as one; then Divine grace will flow into us and bestow contentment in our lives.

We need love for God in order to progress spiritually on the path. Love for God is not just love towards a person, an image or an idol. It is the beginning. Real love for God is loving each and every aspect of creation, seeing the Divinity in everyone and everything.

## 101

If you see an ironsmith working, he will heat and melt a rod and then hit it with a hammer to create the shape he wants. Just as the iron rod must be melted, allow the Guru to melt your heart with love and then shape it with the hammer of knowledge.

Only those who have received love can give love. Hearts of such people who have never received love will always be closed. They will neither be able to receive love or give love. It is very important for parents to give love to the young.

One who is able to love everyone equally is the one who truly loves Amma.

When we understand how trivial our attachments to the world are, and how sublime the love of God is, we will be able to give up all attachments. It is just like flowers on a tree that are withering away so that the tree can bear fruit. When the fruit starts growing, all the flowers automatically drop away.

The love that you experience is proportional to the love that you give.

# 106

Children, all the love that the world offers will ultimately lead to sorrow. There is no selfless love in this world. We believe that we will get happiness from being loved by others, yet happiness is not in any object. It comes from within ourselves. True happiness and eternal peace come only from Divine love, and that Divine love comes only when we see the wholeness of creation.

The ego can only be broken through the pain of love. Just as a seedling can only emerge when the outer shell of the seed breaks open, so too, the Self unfolds when the ego breaks open and disappears. When a conducive atmosphere is created, the potential tree within the seed begins to feel the discomfort of being imprisoned in the shell. It longs to come into the light and be free. It is the intense urge of the dormant tree within that breaks the shell open. There is pain involved in this breaking, but that pain is nothing in relation to the glory of the manifested tree. Once the seedling emerges, the shell becomes insignificant. Similarly, once Self-realisation is attained, the ego loses all significance.

# 108

Untainted, selfless and pure love is the bridge towards God.

CPSIA information can be obtained
at www.ICGtesting.com
Printed in the USA
BVHW03s0127200518
516595BV00006B/21/P

9 781680 377750